Shri Hanuman Aarti & Bhajans

20 Hanuman Prayers in Hindi with English Transliteration

By: Priyal Jhaveri

Published By: My First Picture Book Inc

Index

Index

हनुमान चालीसा

दोहा :

श्रीगुरु चरण सरोज रज
निज मनु मुकुर सुधार
बरनउ रघुवर बिमल जसु
जो दायकु फल चार

बुद्धिहीन तनु जानिके
सुमिरौं पवन कुमार
बल बुद्धि विद्या देहु मोहि
हरहु कलेश विकार

हनुमान चालीसा :

जय हनुमान ज्ञान गुन सागर
जय कपीस तिहुँ लोक उजागर
राम द्रूत अतुलित बल धामा
अंजनि पुत्र पवनसुत नामा

महाबीर बिक्रम बजरंगी
कुमति निवार सुमति के संगी
कंचन बरन बिराज सुबेसा
कानन कुंडल कुँचित केसा

हाथ बज्र औ ध्वजा बिराजे
काँधे मूँज जनेऊ साजे
शंकर सुवन केसरी नंदन
तेज प्रताप महा जगवंदन

विद्यावान गुनी अति चातुर
राम काज करिबे को आतुर
प्रभु चरित्र सुनिबे को रसिया
राम लखन सीता मनबसिया

सूक्ष्म रूप धरि सियहि दिखावा
विकट रूप धरि लंक जरावा
भीम रूप धरि असुर संहारे
रामचंद्र के काज संवारे

लाय सजीवन लखन जियाए
श्री रघुबीर हरषि उर लाए
रघुपति कीन्ही बहुत बढाई
तुम मम प्रिय भरतहि सम भाई

सहस बदन तुम्हरो जस गावै
अस कहि श्रीपति कंठ लगावै
सनकादिक ब्रह्मादि मुनीसा
नारद सारद सहित अहीसा

जम कुबेर दिगपाल जहाँ ते
कवि कोविद कहि सके कहाँ ते
तुम उपकार सुग्रीवहि कीन्हा
राम मिलाय राज पद दीन्हा

तुम्हरो मंत्र विभीषण माना
लंकेश्वर भये सब जग जाना
जुग सहस्त्र जोजन पर भानू
लिल्यो ताहि मधुर फ़ल जानू

प्रभु मुद्रिका मेलि मुख माही
जलधि लाँघि गए अचरज नाही
दुर्गम काज जगत के जेते
सुगम अनुग्रह तुम्हरे तेते

राम दुआरे तुम रखवारे
होत ना आज्ञा बिनु पैसारे
सब सुख लहैं तुम्हारी सरना
तुम रक्षक काहु को डरना

आपन तेज सम्हारो आपै
तीनों लोक हाँक तै कापै
भूत पिशाच निकट नहि आवै
महावीर जब नाम सुनावै

नासै रोग हरे सब पीरा
जपत निरंतर हनुमत बीरा
संकट ते हनुमान छुडावै
मन क्रम वचन ध्यान जो लावै

सब पर राम तपस्वी राजा
तिनके काज सकल तुम साजा
और मनोरथ जो कोई लावै
सोई अमित जीवन फल पावै

चारों जुग परताप तुम्हारा
है परसिद्ध जगत उजियारा
साधु संत के तुम रखवारे
असुर निकंदन राम दुलारे

अष्ट सिद्धि नौ निधि के दाता
अस बर दीन जानकी माता
राम रसायन तुम्हरे पासा
सदा रहो रघुपति के दासा

तुम्हरे भजन राम को पावै
जनम जनम के दुख बिसरावै
अंतकाल रघुवरपुर जाई
जहाँ जन्म हरिभक्त कहाई

और देवता चित्त ना धरई
हनुमत सेई सर्व सुख करई
संकट कटै मिटै सब पीरा
जो सुमिरै हनुमत बलबीरा

जै जै जै हनुमान गुसाईं
कृपा करहु गुरु देव की नाई
जो सत बार पाठ कर कोई
छूटहि बंदि महा सुख होई

जो यह पढ़े हनुमान चालीसा
होय सिद्ध साखी गौरीसा
तुलसीदास सदा हरि चेरा
कीजै नाथ हृदय मह डेरा

पवन तनय संकट हरन
मंगल मूरति रूप
राम लखन सीता सहित
हृदय बसहु सुर भूप

Hanuman Chalisa

Doha :

Shriguru Charan Saroj Raj

Nij Manu Mukur Sudhaar

Baranau Raghuvar Bimal Jasu

Jo Daayaku Phal Chaar

Buddhihin Tanu Jaanike

Sumiraun Pavan Kumaar

Bal Budhi Vidya Dehu Mohi

Harahu Kalesh Vikaar

Hanuman Chalisa :

Jai Hanuman Gyan Gun Sagar
Jay Kapis Tihun Lok Ujaagar
Ram Doot Atulit Bal Dhaama
Anjani Putra Pawansut Naama

Mahaabir Bikram Bajarangi
Kumati Nivaar Sumati Ke Sangi
Kanchan Baran Biraaj Subesa
Kaanan Kundal Kunchit Kesa

Haath Bajr Au Dhvaja Biraaje
Kaandhe Moonj Janeoo Saaje
Shankar Suvan Kesari Nandan
Tej Prataap Maha Jag-Vandan

Vidyaavaan Guni Ati Chaatur

Ram Kaaj Karibe Ko Aatur

Prabhu Charitr Sunibe Ko Rasiya

Ram Lakhan Sita Man-Basiya

Sookshm Roop Dhari Siyahi Dikhaava

Vikat Roop Dhari Lank Jaraava

Bhim Roop Dhari Asur Sanhaare

Raamchandra Ke Kaaj Savaanre

Laay Sajivan Lakhan Jiyaaye

Shri Raghubir Harashi Ur Laaye

Raghupati Kinhi Bahut Badhai

Tum Mam Priy Bharat Hi Sam Bhai

Sahas Badan Tumharo Jas Gaavai

As Kahi Shripati Kanth Lagaavai

Sanakaadik Brahmaadi Munisa

Naarad Saarad Sahit Ahisa

Jam Kuber Digapaal Jahaan Te

Kavi Kovid Kahi Sake Kahaan Te

Tum Upakaar Sugrivahi Kinha

Ram Milaay Raaj Pad Dinha

Tumharo Mantr Vibhishan Maana

Lankesvar Bhaye Sab Jag Jaana

Jug Sahastr Jojan Par Bhaanoo

Lilyo Taahi Madhur Phal Jaanoo

Prabhu Mudrika Meli Mukh Maahi

Jaladhi Laanghi Gae Acharaj Naahi

Durgam Kaaj Jagat Ke Jete

Sugam Anugrah Tumhare Tete

Ram Duaare Tum Rakhavaare

Hot Na Aagya Binu Paisaare

Sab Sukh Lahain Tumhaari Sarana

Tum Rakshak Kaahu Ko Darana

Aapan Tej Samhaaro Aapai

Tinon Lok Haank Tai Kaapai

Bhoot Pishaach Nikat Nahi Aavai

Mahaavir Jab Naam Sunaavai

Naasai Rog Hare Sab Pira

Japat Nirantar Hanumat Bira

Sankat Te Hanuman Chhudaavai

Man Kram Vachan Dhyaan Jo Laavai

Sab Par Ram Tapasvi Raaja

Tinake Kaaj Sakal Tum Saaja

Aur Manorath Jo Koi Laavai

Soi Amit Jivan Phal Paavai

Chaaro Jug Parataap Tumhaara

Hai Parasiddh Jagat Ujiyaara

Saadhu Sant Ke Tum Rakhavaare

Asur Nikandan Ram Dulaare

Asht Siddhi Nau Nidhi Ke Daata

As Bar Din Jaanki Maata

Ram Rasaayan Tumhare Paasa

Sada Raho Raghupati Ke Daasa

Tumhare Bhajan Ram Ko Paavai

Janam Janam Ke Dukh Bisaraavai

Antakaal Raghuvarapur Jai

Jahaan Janm Haribhakt Kahai

Aur Devata Chitt Na Dharahi

Hanumat Sehi Sarv Sukh Karahi

Sankat Katai Mitai Sab Pira

Jo Sumirai Hanumat Balabira

Jai Jai Jai Hanuman Gusain

Krpa Karahu Guru Dev Ki Nai

Jo Sat Baar Paath Kar Koi

Chhootahi Bandi Maha Sukh Hoi

Jo Yah Padhe Hanuman Chalisa

Hoy Siddh Saakhi Gaurisa

Tulasidaas Sada Hari Chera

Kijai Naath Hrday Mah Dera

Pavan Tanay Sankat Haran

Mangal Moorati Roop

Ram Lakhan Sita Sahit

Hrday Basahu Sur Bhoop

हनुमान आरती

आरती कीजै हनुमान लला की
दुष्टदलन रघुनाथ कला की

जाके बल से गिरिवर काँपै
रोग-दोष निकट न झाँपै

अंजनि पुत्र महा बलदाई
संतन के प्रभु सदा सहाई

दे बीरा रघुनाथ पठाये
लंका जारि सीय सुधि लाये

लंका सो कोट समुद्र सी खाई
जात पवनसुत बार न लाई

लंका जारि असुर सँहारे
सियारामजी के काज सँवारे

लक्ष्मण मूर्छित पड़े सकारे
आनि सजीवन प्रान उबारे

पैठि पताल तोरि जम-कारे
अहिरावन की भुजा उखारे

बायें भुजा असुर दल मारे
दहिने भुजा संतजन तारे

सुर नर मुनि आरती उतारे
जै जै जै हनुमान उचारे

कंचन थार कपूर लौ छाई
आरति करत अंजना माई

जो हनुमान जी की आरती गावै
बसि बैकुण्ठ परमपद पावै

आरती कीजै हनुमान लला की
दुष्टदलन रघुनाथ कला की

जाके बल से गिरिवर काँपै
रोग-दोष निकट न झाँपै

Hanuman Aarti

Aarti Kijai Hanuman Lalaa Ki

Dusht-Dalan Raghunath Kalaa Ki

Jaake Bal Se Girivar Kaanpe

Rog-Dosh Nikat Na Jhaanpe

Anjani Putra Maha Baladai

Santan Ke Prabhu Sadaa Sahaai

De Bir Raghunath Pathaaye

Lanka Jaari Siya Sudhi Laaye

Lanka So Kot Samudra Si Khai

Jaat Pavansut Baar Na Lai

Lankaa Jaari Asur Sanhaare

Siya-Ramji Ke Kaaj Sanvaare

Lakshman Moorchhit Pade Sakaare

Aani Sajivan Praan Ubaare

Paithi Pataal Tori Jam-Kaare

Ahiraavan Ki Bhuja Ukhaare

Baaye Bhuja Asur Dal Maare

Dahine Bhuja Santajan Taare

Sur Nar Muni Aarati Utaare

Jai Jai Jai Hanuman Uchaare

Kanchan Thaar Kapoor Lau Chhai

Aarti Karat Anjana Mai

Jo Hanumaan Ji Ki Aarti Gaave

Basi Baikunth Param-Pad Paave

Aarati Kijai Hanuman Lalaa Ki

Dusht-Dalan Raghunath Kalaa Ki

Jaake Bal Se Girivar Kaanpe

Rog-Dosh Nikat Na Jhaanpe

जय जय जय हनुमान गोसाईं

बेगी हरो हनुमान महाप्रभु
जो कछु संकट होए हमारो
कौन से संकट मोर गरीब को
जो तुम से नहीं जात है टारो

जय जय जय हनुमान गोसाईं
कृपा करो महाराज
जय जय जय हनुमान गोसाईं
कृपा करो महाराज

तन मे तुम्हरे शक्ति विराजे
मन भक्ति से भीना
जो जन तुम्हरी शरण मे आये
दुःख दरद हर लीना

महावीर प्रभु हम दुखियन के
तुम हो गरीब नवाज

जय जय जय हनुमान गोसाईं
कृपा करो महाराज

राम लखन वैदेही तुम पर
सदा रहे हर्षाये
हृदय चीर के तुमने
राम सिया का दर्शन दिया कराये

दोऊ कर जोड़ अरज हनुमंता
कहिओ प्रभु से आज

जय जय जय हनुमान गोसाईं
कृपा करो महाराज

राम भजन के तुम हो रसिया
हनुमत मंगलकारी
अर्चन वंदन करते तेरा
दुनिया के नर नारी

राम नाम जप के हनुमंता
बने भगतन सरताज

जय जय जय हनुमान गोसाईं
कृपा करो महाराज
जय जय जय हनुमान गोसाईं
कृपा करो महाराज

Jai Jai Jai Hanuman Gosai

Begi Haro Hanumaan Mahaaprabhu

Jo Kachhu Sankat Hoe Hamaaro

Kaun So Sankat Mor Garib Ko

Jo Tum Se Nahin Jaat Hai Taaro

Jai Jai Jai Hanuman Gosai

Kripa Karo Maharaj

Jai Jai Jai Hanuman Gosai

Kripa Karo Maharaj

Tan Me Tumhare Shakti Viraaje

Man Bhakti Se Bhina

Jo Jan Tumhari Sharan Me Aaye

Dukh Darad Har Lina

Mahaavir Prabhu Ham Dukhiyan Ke

Tum Ho Garib Nawaaj

Jai Jai Jai Hanuman Gosai

Kripa Karo Maharaj

Ram Lakhan Vaidehi Tum Par

Sada Rahe Harshaaye

Hriday Chir Ke Tumane

Ram-Siya Ka Darshan Diya Karaaye

Dou Kar Jod Araj Hanumanta

Kahio Prabhu Se Aaj

Jai Jai Jai Hanuman Gosai

Kripa Karo Maharaj

Ram Bhajan Ke Tum Ho Rasiya

Hanumat Mangalkaari

Archan Vandan Karate Tera

Duniya Ke Nar Naari

Ram Naam Jap Ke Hanumanta

Bane Bhagatan Sartaaj

Jai Jai Jai Hanuman Gosai

Kripa Karo Maharaj

Jai Jai Jai Hanuman Gosai

Kripa Karo Maharaj

मंगल मुरति राम दुलारे

मंगल मुरति राम दुलारे
आन पड़ा अब तेरे द्वारे

मंगल मुरति राम दुलारे
आन पड़ा अब तेरे द्वारे
हे बजरंगबली हनुमान
हे महावीर करो कल्याण

तीनो लोक तेरा उजियारा
दुखिओं का तूने काज सँवारा
हे जगवंदन, केसरी नंदन
कष्ट हरो हे कृपा निधान

मंगल मुरति राम दुलारे
आन पड़ा अब तेरे द्वारे
हे बजरंगबली हनुमान
हे महावीर करो कल्याण

तेरे द्वारे जो भी आया
खाली नहीं कोई लौटाया
दुर्गम काज बनावन हारे
मंगलमय दीजो वरदान

मंगल मुरति राम दुलारे
आन पड़ा अब तेरे द्वारे
हे बजरंगबली हनुमान
हे महावीर करो कल्याण

तेरा सुमिरन हनुमत वीरा
नासे रोग हरे सब पीरा
राम लखन सीता मन बसिया
शरण पड़े का कीजे ध्यान

मंगल मुरति राम दुलारे
आन पड़ा अब तेरे द्वारे
हे बजरंगबली हनुमान
हे महावीर करो कल्याण

मंगल मुरति राम दुलारे
आन पड़ा अब तेरे द्वारे

Mangal Murati Ram Dulare

Mangal Murati Ram Dulare

Aan Pada Ab Tere Dvaare

Mangal Murati Ram Dulare

Aan Pada Ab Tere Dvaare

He Bajarangabali Hanumaan

He Mahaavir Karo Kalyaan

Tino Lok Tera Ujiyaara

Dukhion Ka Toone Kaaj Sanvaara

He Jagavandan, Kesari Nandan

Kasht Haro He Kripa Nidhaan

Mangal Murati Ram Dulare

Aan Pada Ab Tere Dvaare

He Bajarangabali Hanumaan

He Mahaavir Karo Kalyaan

Tere Dvaare Jo Bhi Aaya

Khaali Nahin Koee Lautaaya

Durgam Kaaj Banaavan Haare

Mangalamay Dijo Varadaan

Mangal Murati Ram Dulare

Aan Pada Ab Tere Dvaare

He Bajarangabali Hanumaan

He Mahaavir Karo Kalyaan

Tera Sumiran Hanumat Vira

Naase Rog Hare Sab Pira

Ram Lakhan Sita Man Basiya

Sharan Pade Ka Kije Dhyaan

Mangal Murati Ram Dulare

Aan Pada Ab Tere Dvaare

He Bajarangabali Hanumaan

He Mahaavir Karo Kalyaan

Mangal Murati Ram Dulare

Aan Pada Ab Tere Dvaare

बजरंग बाण

दोहा :

निश्चय प्रेम प्रतीति ते
बिनय करैं सनमान
तेहि के कारज सकल शुभ
सिद्ध करैं हनुमान

चौपाई :

जय हनुमंत संत हितकारी
सुन लीजै प्रभु अरज हमारी
जन के काज बिलंब न कीजै
आतुर दौरि महा सुख दीजै

जैसे कूदि सिंधु के पारा
सुरसा बदन पैठि बिस्तारा
आगे जाय लंकिनी रोका
मारेहु लात गई सुरलोका

जाय बिभीषन को सुख दीन्हा
सीता निरखि परमपद लीन्हा
बाग उजारि सिंधु महँ बोरा
अति आतुर जमकातर तोरा

अक्षय कुमार मारि संहारा
लूम लपेटि लंक को जारा
लाह समान लंक जरि गई
जय जय धुनि सुरपुर नभ भई

अब बिलंब केहि कारन स्वामी
कृपा करहु उर अंतरयामी
जय जय लखन प्रान के दाता
आतुर है दुख करहु निपाता

जै हनुमान जयति बल-सागर
सुर-समूह-समरथ भट-नागर
ॐ हनु हनु हनु हनुमंत हठीले
बैरिहि मारु बज्र की कीले

ॐ ह्रीं ह्रीं ह्रीं हनुमंत कपीसा
ॐ हुं हुं हुं हनु अरि उर सीसा
जय अंजनि कुमार बलवंता
शंकरसुवन बीर हनुमंता

बदन कराल काल-कुल-घालक
राम सहाय सदा प्रतिपालक
भूत, प्रेत, पिसाच निसाचर
अग्नि बेताल काल मारी मर

इन्हें मारु, तोहि सपथ राम की
राखु नाथ मरजाद नाम की
सत्य होहु हरि सपथ पाइ कै
राम दूत धरु मारु धाइ कै

जय जय जय हनुमंत अगाधा
दुख पावत जन केहि अपराधा
पूजा जप तप नेम अचारा
नहिं जानत कछु दास तुम्हारा

बन उपबन मग गिरि गृह माहीं
तुम्हरे बल हौं डरपत नाहीं
जनकसुता हरि दास कहावौ
ताकी सपथ बिलंब न लावौ

जै जै जै धुनि होत अकासा
सुमिरत होय दुसह दुख नासा
चरन पकरि, कर जोरि मनावौं
यहि औसर अब केहि गोहरावौं

उठ, उठ, चलु, तोहि राम दुहाई
पायँ परौं, कर जोरि मनाई
ॐ चं चं चं चं चपल चलंता
ॐ हनु हनु हनु हनु हनुमंता

ॐ हं हं हाँक देत कपि चंचल
ॐ सं सं सहमि पराने खल-दल
अपने जन को तुरत उबारौ
सुमिरत होय आनंद हमारौ

यह बजरंग-बाण जेहि मारै
ताहि कहौ फिरि कवन उबारै
पाठ करै बजरंग-बाण की
हनुमत रक्षा करै प्राण की

यह बजरंग बाण जो जापैं
तासों भूत-प्रेत सब कापैं
धूप देय जो जपै हमेसा
ताके तन नहिं रहै कलेसा

जय हनुमंत संत हितकारी

सुन लीजै प्रभु अरज हमारी

दोहा :

उर प्रतीति दृढ़, सरन है

पाठ करै धरि ध्यान

बाधा सब हर

करैं सब काम सफल हनुमान

Bajrang Baan

Doha :

Nishchay Prem Prateeti Te

Binay Karain Sanmaan

Tehi Ke Kaaraj Sakal Shubh

Siddh Karai Hanuman

Chaupai :

Jai Hanumant Sant Hitkari

Sun Lijai Prabhu Araj Hamaari

Jan Ke Kaaj Bilamb Na Keejai

Aatur Dauri Maha Sukh Deejai

Jaise Koodi Sindhu Ke Paara

Sursaa Badan Paithi Bistaara

Aage Jaay Lankini Roka

Maarehu Laat Gayee Sur-Loka

Jaay Vibhishan Ko Sukh Dinha

Sita Nirakhi Paramapad Linha

Baag Ujaari Sindhu Mahan Bora

Ati Aatur Jamakaatar Tora

Akshay Kumar Maari Sanhaara

Loom Lapeti Lank Ko Jaara

Laah Samaan Lank Jari Gai

Jai Jai Dhuni Surapur Nabh Bhi

Ab Bilamb Kehi Kaaran Svaami

Kripa Karahu Ur Antarayaami

Jai Jai Lakhan Praan Ke Daata

Aatur Hai Dukh Karahu Nipaata

Jai Hanuman Jaiati Bal-Sagar

Sur-Samooh-Samarath Bhat-Naagar

Om Hanu Hanu Hanu Hanumant Hathile

Bairihi Maaru Bajra Ki Kile

Om Hnin Hnin Hnin Hanumant Kapisa

Om Hun Hun Hun Hanu Ari Ur Sisa

Jai Anjani Kumaar Balavanta

Shankar-Suvan Bir Hanumanta

Badan Karaal Kaal-Kul-Ghaalak

Raam Sahaay Sada Pratipaalak

Bhoot, Pret, Pisaach Nisaachar

Agni Betaal Kaal Maari Mar

Inhen Maaru, Tohi Sapath Raam Ki

Raakhu Naath Marajaad Naam Ki

Satya Hohu Hari Sapath Pai Kai

Raam Doot Dharu Maaru Dhai Kai

Jai Jai Jai Hanumant Agaadha

Dukh Paavat Jan Kehi Aparaadha

Pooja Jap Tap Nem Achaara

Nahi Jaanat Kachhu Daas Tumhaara

Ban Upban Mag Giri Grih Maahi

Tumhare Bal Haun Darapat Naahin

Janakasuta Hari Daas Kahaavau

Taaki Sapath Bilamb Na Laavau

Jai Jai Jai Dhuni Hot Akaasa

Sumirat Hoy Dusah Dukh Naasa

Charan Pakari, Kar Jori Manaavaun

Yahi Ausar Ab Kehi Goharaavaun

Uth, Uth, Chalu, Tohi Raam Duhai

Paayan Paraun, Kar Jori Manai

Om Chan Chan Chan Chan Chapal Chalanta

Om Hanu Hanu Hanu Hanu Hanumanta

Om Han Han Haank Det Kapi Chanchal

Om San San Sahami Paraane Khal-Dal

Apane Jan Ko Turat Ubaarau

Sumirat Hoy Aanand Hamaarau

Yah Bajarang-Baan Jehi Maarai

Taaahi Kahau Phiri Kavan Ubaarai

Paath Karai Bajarang-Baan Ki

Hanumat Raksha Karai Praan Ki

Yah Bajarang Baan Jo Jaapain

Taason Bhoot-Pret Sab Kaapain

Dhoop Dey Jo Japai Hamesa

Taake Tan Nahin Rahai Kalesa

Jai Hanumant Sant Hitkari

Sun Lijai Prabhu Araj Hamaari

Doha :

Ur Prateeti Drdh, Saran Hai

Paath Kare Dhari Dhyaan

Baadha Sab Har

Kare Sab Kaam Saphal Hanumaan

भरत भाई, कपि से उरिन हम नाहीं

भरत भाई, कपि से उरिन हम नाहीं
कपि से उरिन हम नाहीं
भरत भाई, कपि से उरिन हम नाहीं

सौ योजन, मर्याद समुद्र की
ये कूदी गयो छन माहीं
लंका जारी, सिया सुधि लायो
पर गर्व नहीं मन माहीं

कपि से उरिन हम नाहीं
भरत भाई, कपि से उरिन हम नाहीं

शक्तिबाण, लग्यो लछमन के
हाहा कार भयो दल माहीं
धौलागिरी, कर धर ले आयो
भोर ना होने पाई

कपि से उरिन हम नाहीं
भरत भाई, कपि से उरिन हम नाहीं

अहिरावन की भुजा उखारी
पैठी गयो मठ माहीं
जो भैया, हनुमत नहीं होते
मोहे, को लातो जग माहीं

कपि से उरिन हम नाहीं
भरत भाई, कपि से उरिन हम नाहीं

आज्ञा भंग, कबहुं नहिं कीन्हीं
जहाँ पठायु तहाँ जाई
तुलसीदास, पवनसुत महिमा
प्रभु निज मुख करत बड़ाई

कपि से उरिन हम नाहीं

भरत भाई, कपि से उरिन हम नाहीं

कपि से उरिन हम नाहीं

भरत भाई, कपि से उरिन हम नाहीं

Bharat Bhai, Kapi Se Urin Hum Nahi

Bharat Bhai, Kapi Se Urin Hum Nahi

Kapi Se Urin Hum Nahi

Bharat Bhai, Kapi Se Urin Hum Naahi

Sau Yojan, Maryaad Samudra Ki

Ye Kudi Gayo Chhan Maahin

Lanka Jaari, Siya Sudhi Laayo

Par Garv Nahin Man Maahin

Kapi Se Urin Hum Nahi

Bharat Bhaai, Kapi Se Uri Hum Nahi

Shakti Baan, Lagyo Lachhaman Ke

Haaha Kaar Bhayo Dal Maahi

Dhaulaagiri, Kar Dhar Le Aayo

Bhor Na Hone Pai

Kapi Se Urin Hum Nahi

Bharat Bhai, Kapi Se Urin Ham Naahi

Ahiraavan Ki Bhuja Ukhaari

Paithi Gayo Math Maahin

Jo Bhaiya, Hanumat Nahin Hote

Mohe, Ko Laato Jag Maahin

Kapi Se Urin Hum Nahi

Bharat Bhai, Kapi Se Urin Hum Naahin

Aagya Bhang, Kabahun Nahin Kinhin

Jahaan Pathaayu Tahaa Jai

Tulasidas, Pavanasut Mahima

Prabhu Nij Mukh Karat Badai

Kapi Se Urin Hum Nahi

Bharat Bhaai Kapee Se Urin Ham Nahi

Kapi Se Urin Hum Nahi

Bharat Bhaai Kapi Se Urin Hum Nahi

बजरंगबली मेरी नाव चली

बजरंगबली मेरी नाव चली
बजरंगबली मेरी नाव चली
मेरी नाव को पार लगा देना

मुझे माया मोह ने घेर लिया
मुझे माया मोह ने घेर लिया
संताप हृदय का मिटा देना

बजरंगबली मेरी नाव चली

मैं दास तो आपका जन्म से हूँ
मैं दास तो आपका जन्म से हूँ
बालक और शिष्य भी धर्म से हूँ
बालक और शिष्य भी धर्म से हूँ

निर्लज विमुख निज कर्म से हूँ
निर्लज विमुख निज कर्म से हूँ
चित में मेरा दोष भुला देना

बजरंगबली मेरी नाव चली
मेरी नाव को पार लगा देना

दुर्बल गरीब और दीन भी हूँ
दुर्बल गरीब और दीन भी हूँ
निज कर्म क्रिया गत क्षिद्र भी हूँ
निज कर्म क्रिया गत क्षिद्र भी हूँ

बलवीर तेरे आधीन हूँ मैं
बलवीर तेरे आधीन हूँ मैं
मेरी बिगड़ी बात बना देना

बजरंगबली मेरी नाव चली
मेरी नाव को पार लगा देना

बल मुझको दे निर्भय कर दो
बल मुझको दे निर्भय कर दो
यश शक्ति मेरी अक्षय कर दो
यश शक्ति मेरी अक्षय कर दो

मेरा जीवन अमृतमय कर दो
मेरा जीवन अमृतमय कर दो
संजीवनी मुझे पिला देना

बजरंगबली मेरी नाव चली
मेरी नाव को पार लगा देना

करूणानिधि नाम तो आपका है
करूणानिधि नाम तो आपका है
तुम रामदूत अभिराम प्रभु

छोटा सा है एक काम मेरा
श्री राम से मोहे मिला देना

बजरंगबली मेरी नाव चली
मेरी नाव को पार लगा देना

बजरंगबली मेरी नाव चली
बजरंगबली मेरी नाव चली
मेरी नाव को पार लगा देना

मुझे माया मोह ने घेर लिया
मुझे माया मोह ने घेर लिया
संताप ह्रदय का मिटा देना

बजरंगबली मेरी नाव चली
बजरंगबली मेरी नाव चली

Bajrangbali Meri Naav Chali

Bajrang Bali Meri Naav Chali

Bajrang Bali Meri Naav Chali

Meri Naav Ko Paar Laga Dena

Mujhe Maya Moh Ne Gher Liya

Mujhe Maya Moh Ne Gher Liya

Santaap Hriday Ka Mita Dena

Bajrang Bali Meri Nav Chali

Mai Das To Aapka Janam Se Hu

Mai Das To Aapka Janam Se Hu

Balak Aur Shishya Bhi Dharm Se Hoo

Balak Aur Shishya Bhi Dharm Se Hoo

Nirlajja Vimukh Nij Karma Se Hu

Nirlajja Vimukh Nij Karma Se Hu

Chit Se Mera Dosh Bhula Dena

Bajrang Bali Meri Naav Chali

Meri Naav Ko Paar Lagaa Denaa

Durbal Garib Aur Deen Bhi Hu

Durbal Garib Aur Deen Bhi Hu

Nij Karma Kriya Gat Ksheed Bhi Hu

Nij Karma Kriya Gat Ksheed Bhi Hu

Balbeer Tere Adheen Hu Mai

Balbeer Tere Adheen Hu Mai

Meri Bigadi Baat Bana Dena

Bajrang Bali Meri Nav Chali

Meri Naav Ko Paar Laga Dena

Bal Mujhko De Nirbhay Kardo

Bal Mujhko De Nirbhay Kardo

Yash Shakti Meri Akshay Kardo

Yash Shakti Meri Akshay Kardo

Mera Jeevan Amratmay Kardo

Mera Jeevan Amratmay Kardo

Sanjeevani Mujhe Pila Dena

Bajrang Bali Meri Naav Chalee

Meri Naav Ko Paar Lagaa Dena

Karuna Nidhi Naam To Aapka Hai

Karuna Nidhi Naam To Aapka Hai

Tum Raam Doot Aviraam Prabhu

Chhota Sa Hai Ek Kaam Mera

Shri Ram Se Mohe Mila Dena

Bajrang Bali Meri Nav Chalee

Meri Naav Ko Paar Laga Dena

Bajrang Bali Meri Naav Chali

Bajrang Bali Meri Nav Chali

Meri Naav Ko Paar Laga Dena

Mujhe Maya Moh Ne Gher Liya

Mujhe Maya Moh Ne Gher Liyaa

Santaap Harday Ka Mita Dena

Bajrang Bali Meri Naav Chali

Bajrang Bali Meri Naav Chali

जय हो जय हो तुम्हारी जी बजरंगबली

जय हो जय हो तुम्हारी जी बजरंगबली
ले के शिव रूप आना गज़ब हो गया
त्रेता युग में थे, तुम आये द्वापर में भी
तेरा कलयुग में आना गज़ब हो गया

जय हो
जय हो जय हो तुम्हारी जी बजरंगबली

बचपन की कहानी निराली बड़ी
जब लगी भूख बजरंग मचलने लगे
फल समझ कर उड़े आप आकाश में
तेरा सूरज को खाना गज़ब हो गया

जय हो जय हो तुम्हारी जी बजरंगबली
ले के शिव रूप आना गज़ब हो गया

कूदे लंका में जब मच गयी खलबली
मारे चुन चुन के असुरों को बजरंगबली
मार डाले अक्षय को पटक कर वही
तेरा लंका जलाना गज़ब हो गया

जय हो जय हो तुम्हारी जी बजरंगबली
ले के शिव रूप आना गज़ब हो गया

आके शक्ति लगी जो लखन लाल को
राम जी देख रोये लखन लाल को
लेके संजीवन बूटी पवन वेग से
पूरा पर्वत उठाना गज़ब हो गया

जय हो जय हो तुम्हारी जी बजरंगबली
ले के शिव रूप आना गज़ब हो गया

जब विभिषण संग बैठे थे श्री रामजी
और चरणों में हाजिर थे हनुमानजी
सुन के ताना विभिषण का अंजनी के लाल
फाड़ सीना दिखाना गज़ब हो गया

जय हो जय हो तुम्हारी जी बजरंगबली
ले के शिव रूप आना गज़ब हो गया

Jai Ho Jai Ho Tumhari Ji Bajrangbali

Jai Ho Jai Ho Tumhari Ji Bajrang Bali

Le Ke Shiv Roop Aana Gazab Ho Gaya

Treta Yug Mein The, Tum Aaye Dwapar Mein Bhi

Tera Kalayug Mein Aana Gazab Ho Gaya

Jay Ho

Jai Ho Jai Ho Tumhari Ji Bajrang Bali

Bachapan Ki Kahaani Niraali Badi

Jab Lagi Bhookh Bajarang Machalane Lage

Phal Samajh Kar Ude Aap Aakaash Mein

Tera Suraj Ko Khaana Gazab Ho Gaya

Jai Ho Jai Ho Tumhari Ji Bajrang Bali

Le Ke Shiv Roop Aana Gazab Ho Gaya

Koode Lanka Mein Jab Mach Gayi Khalabali

Maare Chun Chun Ke Asuron Ko Bajarang-Bali

Maar Daale Akshay Ko Patak Kar Vahi

Tera Lanka Jalaana Gazab Ho Gaya

Jai Ho Jai Ho Tumhari Ji Bajrang Bali

Le Ke Shiv Roop Aana Gazab Ho Gaya

Aake Shakti Lagi Jo Lakhan Laal Ko

Ramji Dekh Roye Lakhan Laal Ko

Leke Sanjivan Booti Pavan Veg Se

Poora Parvat Uthaana Gazab Ho Gaya

Jai Ho Jai Ho Tumhari Ji Bajrang Bali

Le Ke Shiv Roop Aana Gazab Ho Gaya

Jab Vibhishan Sang Baithe The Shri Ramji

Aur Charano Mein Haajir The Hanumanji

Sun Ke Taana Vibhishan Ka Anjani Ke Laal

Phaad Sina Dikhaana Gazab Ho Gaya

Jai Ho Jai Ho Tumhari Ji Bajrang Bali

Le Ke Shiv Roop Aana Gazab Ho Gaya

आजा हनुमान प्यारे, व्याकुल है रघुवीरा

आजा हनुमान प्यारे
व्याकुल है रघुवीरा

आजा हनुमान प्यारे
व्याकुल है रघुवीरा

मूर्छित लखन जी हुए
कैसी विपदा आई रे
बूटी जल्दी तुम लाओ
हनुमत गोसाई
होवे न अब सवेरा

आजा हनुमान प्यारे
व्याकुल है रघुवीरा

भीगे श्री राम के नैना
रोये सब सेना
बोले बजरंग प्रभु से
सुख से बीते रैना हो

दूर मैं करूंगा पीड़ा
आजा हनुमान प्यारे
व्याकुल है रघुवीरा

तेज गति से उड़के
द्रोणा गिरी आये
बूटी समज ना आये
पर्वत ही लाये हो

तुम हो बलबीरा
आजा हनुमान प्यारे
व्याकुल है रघुवीरा

लक्ष्मण जी के प्राण बचाये

राम हरषाये हो

प्यारे भक्त राम जी के

आप ही कहलाये हो

जय जय महावीरा

आजा हनुमान प्यारे

व्याकुल है रघुवीरा

आजा हनुमान प्यारे

व्याकुल है रघुवीरा

Aja Hanuman Pyare Vyakul Hai Raghuveera

Aja Hanuman Pyare

Vyakul Hai Raghuveera

Aja Hanuman Pyare

Vyakul Hai Raghuveera

Moorchhit Lakhanji Huye

Kaisi Vipada Aai Re

Booti Jaldi Tum Lao

Hanumat Gosai

Hove Na Ab Savera

Aaja Hanumaan Pyaare

Vyakul Hai Raghuveera

Bhige Shri Ram Ke Naina

Roye Sab Sena

Bole Bajarang Prabhu Se

Sukh Se Bite Raina Ho

Door Main Karoonga Peeda

Aaja Hanumaan Pyaare

Vyaakul Hai Raghuveera

Tej Gati Se Ud Ke

Drona Giri Aaye

Booti Samaj Na Aaye

Parvat Hi Laaye Ho

Tum Ho Balabira

Aja Hanuman Pyare

Vyakul Hai Raghuveera

Lakshmanji Ke Praan Bachaaye

Raam Harashaaye Ho

Pyaare Bhakt Raamji Ke

Aap Hi Kahalaaye Ho

Jay Jay Mahaavira

Aaja Hanumaan Pyaare

Vyakul Hai Raghuveera

Aaja Hanumaan Pyaare

Vyakul Hai Raghuveera

बोले बोले हनुमान बोलो

बोल बजरंग बलि की जय
बोल पवन पुत्र हनुमान की जय

बोले बोले हनुमान
बोलो भक्तो सिया राम
श्री राम के चरणों में
बनते बिगड़े काम

बोले बोले हनुमान
बोलो भक्तो सिया राम
बोले बोले हनुमान
बोलो भक्तो सिया राम

उसकी शोभा है विष्णु में
उसकी शोभा है मोहन सी
तुलसी ने जब शीश झुकाया
धनुष बनी कान्हा की बंसी

राम की माया राम ही जाने
कण कण में श्री राम

बोले बोले हनुमान
बोलो भक्तो सिया राम
श्री राम के चरणों में
बनते बिगड़े काम

लिपट लिपट के राम चरण
आँखों में गंगा जल भर ले
श्री राम तो क्षमा शील है
पापो को स्वीकार तू करले

श्री राम के चरण कमल
जैसे बैकुंठ धाम

बोले बोले हनुमान
बोलो भक्तो सिया राम
श्री राम के चरणों में
बनते बिगड़े काम

बोले बोले हनुमान
बोलो भक्तो सिया राम

बोल बोल तू राम रमैया
जीवन फिर न मिलेगा भैया
दुनिया तो भ्रम जाल है मुरख
राम ही पार लगाये नैय्या

राघव के चरणों में
पायेगा तू विश्राम

बोले बोले हनुमान
बोलो भक्तो सिया राम
श्री राम के चरणों में
बनते बिगड़े काम

बोले बोले हनुमान
बोलो भक्तो सिया राम

बोल बजरंग बलि की जय
बोल पवन पुत्र हनुमान की जय

बोले बोले हनुमान
बोलो भक्तो सिया राम
श्री राम के चरणों में
बनते बिगड़े काम

बोले बोले हनुमान
बोलो भक्तो सिया राम

बोले बोले हनुमान
बोलो भक्तो सिया राम
श्री राम के चरणों में
बनते बिगड़े काम

बोले बोले हनुमान
बोलो भक्तो सिया राम

Bole Bole Hanuman Bolo

Bol Bajarang Bali Ki Jay

Bol Pavan Putra Hanuman Ki Jay

Bole Bole Hanuman

Bolo Bhakto Siya Ram

Shri Ram Ke Charano Mein

Banate Bigade Kaam

Bole Bole Hanuman

Bolo Bhakto Siya Ram

Bole Bole Hanuman

Bolo Bhakto Siya Ram

Usaki Shobha Hai Vishnu Mein

Usaki Shobha Hai Mohan Si

Tulsi Ne Jab Shish Jhukaaya

Dhanush Bani Kaanha Ki Bansi

Ram Ki Maaya Ram Hi Jaane

Kan Kan Mein Shri Ram

Bole Bole Hanuman

Bolo Bhakto Siyaram

Shri Ram Ke Charanon Mein

Banate Bigade Kaam

Lipat Lipat Ke Ram Charan

Aankhon Mein Ganga Jal Bhar Le

Shri Ram To Kshama Shil Hai

Paapo Ko Svikaar Tu Karale

Shri Ram Ke Charan Kamal

Jaise Baikunth Dhaam

Bole Bole Hanuman

Bolo Bhakto Siya Ram

Shri Ram Ke Charanon Mein

Banate Bigade Kaam

Bole Bole Hanuman

Bolo Bhakto Siya Ram

Bol Bol Tu Ram Ramaiya

Jivan Phir Na Milega Bhaiya

Duniya To Bhram Jaal Hai Murakh

Ram Hi Paar Lagaaye Naiyya

Raaghav Ke Charanon Mein

Paayega Tu Vishraam

Bole Bole Hanuman

Bolo Bhakto Siya Ram

Shri Ram Ke Charanon Mein

Banate Bigade Kaam

Bole Bole Hanuman

Bolo Bhakto Siya Ram

Bol Bajarang Bali Ki Jay

Bol Pavan Putr Hanuman Ki Jay

Bole Bole Hanuman

Bolo Bhakto Siya Ram

Shri Ram Ke Charanon Mein

Banate Bigade Kaam

Bole Bole Hanuman

Bolo Bhakto Siya Ram

Bole Bole Hanuman

Bolo Bhakto Siya Ram

Shri Ram Ke Charanon Mein

Banate Bigade Kaam

Bole Bole Hanuman

Bolo Bhakto Siya Ram

आओ हनुमान जी मेरे घर

आओ हनुमान जी मेरे घर
पूरी कर दो प्रभु आस मेरी
कर दो मुझपे दया की नजर
पूरी कर दो प्रभु आस मेरी

याद कर लो प्रभु उस घड़ी को
दर्श दिया गणेश पूरी को
बाबा ने समाधी लगाई
सेवा दी जब किशोर पूरी को

किया मोहन को तुमने अमर
पूरी कर दो प्रभु आस मेरी
आओ हनुमान जी मेरे घर
पूरी कर दो प्रभु आस मेरी

तुम्हे ढूंढा कभी सालासार में
कभी खोजा तुम्हे महेंदीपुर में
जितने थे धाम मेरी नजर में
मैंने ढूंढा तुम्हे दुनिया भर में

खोजते बीती जाए उमर
पूरी कर दो प्रभु आस मेरी
आओ हनुमान जी मेरे घर
पूरी कर दो प्रभु आस मेरी

जपते जपते प्रभु बाला बाला
थक गई मैं तो अंजनी लाला
ताने देते है दुनिया वाले
लाज रख लो प्रभु घाटेवाले

वैरागी विनय तू भी कर
पूरी कर दो प्रभु आस मेरी
आओ हनुमान जी मेरें घर
पूरी कर दो प्रभु आस मेरी

कर दो मुझपे दया की नजर
पूरी कर दो प्रभु आस मेरी
आओ हनुमान जी मेरे घर
पूरी कर दो प्रभु आस मेरी

Aao Hanumanji Mere Ghar

Aao Hanumanji Mere Ghar

Poori Kar Do Prabhu Aas Meri

Kar Do Mujh Pe Daya Ki Najar

Poori Kar Do Prabhu Aas Meri

Yaad Kar Lo Prabhu Us Ghadi Ko

Darsh Diya Ganesh Poori Ko

Baba Ne Samadhi Lagayee

Seva Di Jab Kishor Poori Ko

Kiya Mohan Ko Tum Ne Amar

Poori Kar Do Prabhu Aas Meri

Aao Hanumanji Mere Ghar

Poori Kar Do Prabhu Aas Meri

Tumhe Dhundha Kabhi Saalaasaar Mein

Kabhi Khoja Tumhe Mahendipur Mein

Jit Ne The Dhaam Meri Najar Mein

Maine Dhoondha Tumhe Duniya Bhar Mein

Khojate Biti Jaaye Umar

Poori Kar Do Prabhu Aas Meri

Aao Hanumanji Mere Ghar

Poori Kar Do Prabhu Aas Meri

Japate Japate Prabhu Baala Baala

Thak Gai Main To Anjani Laala

Taane Dete Hai Duniya Vaale

Laaj Rakh Lo Prabhu Ghaatevaale

Vairaagi Vinay Too Bhi Kar

Poori Kar Do Prabhu Aas Meri

Aao Hanumanji Mere Ghar

Poori Kar Do Prabhu Aas Meri

Kar Do Mujh Pe Daya Ki Najar

Poori Kar Do Prabhu Aas Meri

Aao Hanumanji Mere Ghar

Poori Kar Do Prabhu Aas Meri

आना पवन कुमार

आना पवन कुमार
हमारे हरी कीर्तन में
आना पवन कुमार
हमारे हरी कीर्तन में

बाबा आना अंजनी के लाल
हमारे हरी कीर्तन में
आना पवन कुमार
हमारे हरी कीर्तन में

आप भी आना संग में राम जी को लाना
आप भी आना, बाबा आप भी आना
हो बजरंग आप भी आना
आप भी आना संग में राम जी को लाना

लाना, लाना, लाना जनक दुलार
हमारे हरी कीर्तन में
लाना जनक दुलार
हमारे हरी कीर्तन में

बाबा आना पवन कुमार
हमारे हरी कीर्तन में

भरत जी को लाना, लक्ष्मण जी को लाना
भरत जी को लाना, लक्ष्मण जी को लाना

लाना, लाना, लाना सब परिवार
हमारे हरी कीर्तन में
लाना सब परिवार
हमारे हरी कीर्तन में

आना पवन कुमार
हमारे हरी कीर्तन में

कृष्ण जी को लाना, राधा जी को लाना
कृष्ण जी को लाना, बाबा कृष्ण जी को लाना
कृष्ण जी को लाना और राधा जी को लाना

लाना, लाना, लाना भक्त दातार
हमारे हरी कीर्तन में
लाना भक्त दातार
हमारे हरी कीर्तन में

बाबा आना पवन कुमार
हमारे हरी कीर्तन में

शिव जी को लाना, मैया जी को लाना
शिव जी को लाना
शिव जी को लाना, मैया जी को लाना

लाना, लाना, लाना मदन मुरार
हमारे हरी कीर्तन में
लाना मदन मुरार
हमारे हरी कीर्तन में

आजा
आना पवन कुमार
हमारे हरी कीर्तन में

सुमति को लाना, कुमति को हटाना
सुमति को लाना, कुमति को हटाना
करना, करना, करना बेडा पार
हमारे हरी कीर्तन में
करना बेडा पार
हमारे हरी कीर्तन में

बाबा आना पवन कुमार
हमारे हरी कीर्तन में

कावड़ संग पर कृपा करके

कावड़ संग पे बाबा कावड़ संग पे

बजरंग कावड़ संग पे

कावड़ संग पे कृपा करके

सुनलो, सुनलो, सुनलो मेरी पुकार

हमारे हरी कीर्तन में

सुनलो मेरी पुकार हमारे हरी कीर्तन में

आजा...

आजा पवन कुमार

हमारे हरी कीर्तन में

आना अंजनी के लाल

हमारे हरी कीर्तन में

आजा...

आजा पवन कुमार

हमारे हरी कीर्तन में

आना अंजनी के लाल

हमारे हरी कीर्तन में

Aana Pawan Kumar

Aana Pawan Kumar

Hamare Hari Kirtan Me

Aana Pawan Kumar

Hamare Hari Kirtan Me

Baba Aana Anjani Ke Laal

Hamare Hari Kirtan Me

Aana Pawan Kumar

Hamare Hari Kirtan Me

Aap Bhi Aana Sang Mein Ramji Ko Laana

Aap Bhi Aana, Baaba Aap Bhi Aana

Ho Bajarang Aap Bhi Aana

Aap Bhi Aana Sang Mein Ramji Ko Laana

Laana, Laana, Laana Janak Dulaar

Hamare Hari Kirtan Me

Laana Janak Dulaar

Hamare Hari Kirtan Me

Baaba Aana Pawan Kumar

Hamare Hari Kirtan Me

Bharatji Ko Laana, Lakshmanji Ko Laana

Bharatji Ko Laana, Laxmanji Ko Laana

Laana, Laana, Laana Sab Parivaar

Hamare Hari Kirtan Me

Laana Sab Parivaar

Hamare Hari Kirtan Me

Aana Pawan Kumar

Hamare Hari Kirtan Me

Krshnji Ko Laana, Radhaji Ko Laana

Krshnji Ko Laana, Baaba Krshnji Ko Laana

Krshnji Ko Laana Aur Radhaji Ko Laana

Laana, Laana, Laana Bhakt Daataar

Hamare Hari Kirtan Me

Laana Bhakt Daataar

Hamare Hari Kirtan Me

Baaba Aana Pawan Kumar

Hamare Hari Kirtan Me

Shivji Ko Laana, Maiyaji Ko Laana

Shivji Ko Laana

Shivji Ko Laana, Maiyaji Ko Laana

Laana, Laana, Laana Madan Muraar

Hamare Hari Kirtan Me

Laana Madan Muraar

Hamare Hari Kirtan Me

Aaja

Aana Pawan Kumar

Hamare Hari Kirtan Me

Sumati Ko Laana, Kumati Ko Hataana

Sumati Ko Laana, Kumati Ko Hataana

Karana, Karana, Karana Beda Paar

Hamare Hari Kirtan Me

Karana Beda Paar

Hamare Hari Kirtan Me

Baaba Aana Pawan Kumar

Hamare Hari Kirtan Me

Kaavad Sang Par Krpa Karake

Kaavad Sang Pe Baaba Kaavad Sang Pe

Bajarang Kaavad Sang Pe

Kaavad Sang Pe Krpa Karake

Sunalo, Sunalo, Sunalo Meri Pukaar

Hamare Hari Kirtan Me

Sunalo Meri Pukaar Hamare Hari Kirtan Me

Aaja ...

Aaja Pavan Kumaar

Hamare Hari Kirtan Me

Aana Anjani Ke Laal

Hamare Hari Kirtan Me

Aaja ...

Aaja Pavan Kumaar

Hamare Hari Kirtan Me

Aana Anjani Ke Laal

Hamare Hari Kirtan Me

दुनिया मे देव हजारो हैं

दुनिया मे देव हजारो हैं
बजरंग बली का क्या कहना

इनकी शक्ति का क्या कहना
इनकी भक्ति का क्या कहना

दुनिया मे देव हजारो हैं
बजरंग बली का क्या कहना

ये सात समुन्दर लांघ गए
ये गढ़ लंका मे कूद गए

रावण को डराना क्या कहना
लंका को जलाना क्या कहना

इनकी शक्ति का क्या कहना
इनकी भक्ति का क्या कहना
दुनिया मे देव हजारो हैं
बजरंग बली का क्या कहना

जब लक्ष्मन जी बेहोश हुए
संजीवनी बूटी लाने गए

परबत को उठाना क्या कहना
लक्ष्मन को जिलाना क्या कहना

इनकी शक्ति का क्या कहना
इनकी भक्ति का क्या कहना
दुनिया मे देव हजारो हैं
बजरंग बली का क्या कहना

भक्तो इनके सीने मे
सिया राम की जोड़ी बैठी है

ये राम दिवाना क्या कहना
गुण गाये जमाना क्या कहना

इनकी शक्ति का क्या कहना
इनकी भक्ति का क्या कहना

दुनिया मे देव हजारो हैं
बजरंग बली का क्या कहना

दुनिया मे देव हजारो हैं
बजरंग बली का क्या कहना

Duniya Me Dev Hazaro Hai

Duniya Me Dev Hazaro Hai

Bajrangbali Ka Kya Kehna

Inaki Shakti Ka Kya Kahana

Inaki Bhakti Ka Kya Kahana

Duniya Me Dev Hazaro Hai

Bajrangbali Ka Kya Kehna

Ye Saat Samundar Laangh Gae

Ye Gadh Lanka Me Kood Gae

Raavan Ko Daraana Kya Kahana

Lanka Ko Jalaana Kya Kahana

Inaki Shakti Ka Kya Kahanaa

Inaki Bhakti Ka Kya Kahanaa

Duniya Me Dev Hazaaro Hai

Bajrangbali Ka Kya Kehna

Jab Lakshmanji Behosh Huye

Sanjivani Booti Laane Gae

Parabat Ko Uthaana Kya Kahana

Lakshman Ko Jilaana Kya Kahana

Inaki Shakti Ka Kyaa Kahana

Inaki Bhakti Ka Kyaa Kahana

Duniyaa Mein Dev Hazaro Hai

Bajrang Bali Ka Kya Kehna

Bhakto Inake Sine Me

Siyaram Ki Jodi Baithi Hai

Ye Ram Diwaana Kya Kahanaa

Gun Gaaye Jamaana Kya Kahana

Inaki Shakti Ka Kya Kahana

Inaki Bhakti Ka Kya Kahana

Duniya Me Dev Hazaro Hai

Bajrangbali Ka Kya Kehna

Duniya Me Dev Hazaro Hai

Bajrangbali Ka Kya Kehna

दुनिया रचने वाले को

दुनिया रचने वाले को भगवान कहते हैं
संकट हरने वाले को हनुमान कहते हैं

दुनिया रचने वाले को भगवान कहते हैं
संकट हरने वाले को हनुमान कहते हैं

हो जाते है जिसके अपने पराये
हनुमान उसको कंठ लगाये

जब रूठ जाये संसार सारा
बजरंगबली तब देते सहारा

अपने भक्तो का बजरंगी मान करते है
संकट हरने वाले को हनुमान कहते हैं

दुनिया रचने वाले को भगवान कहते हैं
और संकट हरने वाले को हनुमान कहते हैं

दुनिया में काम कोई ऐसा नहीं है
हनुमान के जो बस में नहीं है

जो चीज मांगो, पल में मिलेगी
झोली ये खाली खुशियों से भरेगी

सच्चे मन से जो भी इनका ध्यान करते है
संकट हरने वाले को हनुमान कहते हैं

दुनिया रचने वाले को भगवान कहते हैं
और संकट हरने वाले को हनुमान कहते हैं

कट जाये संकट इनकी शरण में
बैठ के देखो बजरंग के चरण में

भक्त की बातों को झूठ मत मानो
फिर ना फंसोगे जीवन मरण में

और देवता चित्त ना धरही
हनुमंत से सर्व सुख करही

इनके सीने में हरदम सिया राम रहते है
संकट हरने वाले को हनुमान कहते हैं

दुनिया रचने वाले को भगवान कहते हैं
संकट हरने वाले को हनुमान कहते हैं

संकट कटे मिटे सब पीरा
जो सुमिरै हनुमत बल बीरा

दुनिया रचने वाले को भगवान कहते हैं
संकट हरने वाले को हनुमान कहते हैं

Duniya Rachne Wale Ko

Duniya Rachne Wale Ko Bhagwan Kehte Hai

Sankat Harne Wale Ko Hanuman Kehte Hain

Duniya Rachne Wale Ko Bhagwan Kehte Hain

Sankat Harne Wale Ko Hanuman Kehte Hain

Ho Jaate Hai Jisake Apane Paraaye

Hanuman Usko Kanth Lagaaye

Jab Rooth Jaaye Sansaar Saara

Bajarangbali Tab Dete Sahaara

Apne Bhakto Ka Bajarangi Maan Karate Hai

Sankat Harne Wale Ko Hanuman Kehte Hain

Duniya Rachne Wale Ko Bhagwan Kehte Hai

Aur Sankat Harne Wale Ko Hanuman Kehte Hain

Duniya Mein Kaam Koi Aisa Nahin Hai

Hanuman Ke Jo Bas Mein Nahin Hai

Jo Cheej Maango, Pal Mein Milegi

Jholi Ye Khaali Khushiyon Se Bharegi

Sachche Man Se Jo Bhi Inka Dhyaan Karate Hai

Sankat Harne Wale Ko Hanuman Kehte Hain

Duniya Rachne Wale Ko Bhagwan Kehte Hai

Aur Sankat Harne Wale Ko Hanuman Kehte Hain

Kat Jaaye Sankat Inki Sharan Mein

Baith Ke Dekho Bajarang Ke Charan Mein

Bhakt Ki Baaton Ko Jhooth Mat Maano

Phir Na Phansoge Jivan Maran Mein

Aur Devta Chitt Na Dharai

Hanumant Se Sarv Sukh Karai

Inke Siney Mein Hardam Siya Ram Rahate Hai

Sankat Harne Wale Ko Hanuman Kehte Hain

Duniya Rachne Wale Ko Bhagwan Kehte Hai

Sankat Harne Wale Ko Hanuman Kehte Hain

Sankat Kate Mite Sab Pira

Jo Sumirai Hanumat Bal Bira

Duniya Rachne Wale Ko Bhagwan Kehte Hai

Sankat Harne Wale Ko Hanuman Kehte Hain

कलयुग मे सिद्ध हो देव तुम्ही हनुमान

कलयुग मे सिद्ध हो देव तुम्ही
हनुमान तुम्हारा क्या कहना
तेरी शक्ति का क्या कहना
तेरी भक्ति का क्या कहना

सीता की खोज करी तुमने
तुम सात समन्दर पार गये
लंका को किया शमशान प्रभु
बलवान तुम्हारा क्या कहना

तेरी भक्ति का क्या कहना
तेरी शक्ति का क्या कहना
कलयुग मे सिद्ध हो देव तुम्ही
हनुमान तुम्हारा क्या कहना

जब लक्ष्मनजी को शक्ति लगी
तुम धौलागिर पर्वत लाये
लक्ष्मण के बचाये आ कर के
तब प्राण तुम्हारा क्या कहना

तेरी भक्ति का क्या कहना
तेरी शक्ति का क्या कहना
कलयुग मे सिद्ध हो देव तुम्ही
हनुमान तुम्हारा क्या कहना

तुम भक्त शिरोमनी हो जग मे
तुम वीर शिरोमनी हो जग मे
तेरे रोम रोम मे बसते हैं
सिया राम तुम्हारा क्या कहना

तेरी भक्ति का क्या कहना
तेरी शक्ति का क्या कहना
कलयुग मे सिद्ध हो देव तुम्ही
हनुमान तुम्हारा क्या कहना

कलयुग मे सिद्ध हो देव तुम्ही
हनुमान तुम्हारा क्या कहना

Kalyug Me Siddh Ho Dev Tumhi Hanuman

Kalayug Me Siddh Ho Dev Tumhi

Hanuman Tumhaara Kya Kahana

Teri Shakti Ka Kya Kahana

Teri Bhakti Ka Kya Kahana

Sita Ki Khoj Kari Tum Ne

Tum Saat Samandar Paar Gaye

Lanka Ko Kiya Shamashaan Prabhu

Balavaan Tumhaara Kya Kahana

Teri Bhakti Ka Kya Kahana

Teri Shakti Ka Kya Kahana

Kalayug Me Siddh Ho Dev Tumhi

Hanuman Tumhaara Kya Kahana

Jab Lakshmanji Ko Shakti Lagi

Tum Dhaulaagir Parvat Laaye

Lakshman Ke Bachaaye Aa Kar Ke

Tab Praan Tumhaara Kya Kahana

Teri Bhakti Ka Kya Kahana

Teri Shakti Ka Kya Kahana

Kalayug Me Siddh Ho Dev Tumhi

Hanuman Tumhaara Kya Kahana

Tum Bhakt Shiromani Ho Jag Me

Tum Vir Shiromani Ho Jag Me

Tere Rom Rom Me Basate Hain

Siya Raam Tumhaara Kya Kahana

Teri Bhakti Ka Kya Kahana

Teri Shakti Ka Kya Kahana

Kalayug Me Siddh Ho Dev Tumhi

Hanuman Tumhaara Kya Kahana

Kalayug Me Siddh Ho Dev Tumhi

Hanuman Tumhaara Kya Kahana

दुनिया के मालिक को भगवान कहते हैं

दुनिया के मालिक को भगवान कहते हैं
दुनिया के मालिक को भगवान कहते हैं
संकट के साथी को हनुमान कहते हैं
संकट के साथी को हनुमान कहते हैं

दुनिया के मालिक को भगवान कहते हैं
संकट के साथी को हनुमान कहते हैं

जब रिश्तेदार तुमसे मुखड़ा छुपाए
हनुमान तेरा साथ निभाए

हनुमान तेरा साथ निभाए
हनुमान तेरा साथ निभाए

जब दुनिया वाले दें ना सहारा
हनुमान पकड़े दामन तुम्हारा

हनुमान पकड़े दामन तुम्हारा
हनुमान पकड़े दामन तुम्हारा

पढ़ लो सारे
पढ़ लो सारे वेद और पुराण कहते हैं
पढ़ लो सारे वेद और पुराण कहते हैं

संकट के साथी को हनुमान कहते हैं
संकट के साथी को हनुमान कहते हैं

दुनिया के मालिक को भगवान कहते हैं
दुनिया के मालिक को भगवान कहते हैं
संकट के साथी को हनुमान कहते हैं
संकट के साथी को हनुमान कहते हैं

जो काम इसके वश में नहीं है
एक काम हमको ऐसा बता दो

एक काम हमको ऐसा बता दो

एक काम हमको ऐसा बता दो

हनुमान खुश हो जाएगा तुमसे

बस इनको थोड़ा सिंदूर लगा दो

बस इनको थोड़ा सिंदूर लगा दो

बस इनको थोड़ा सिंदूर लगा दो

दुनिया के

दुनिया के सारे इंसान कहते हैं

दुनिया के सारे इंसान कहते हैं

संकट के साथी को हनुमान कहते हैं

संकट के साथी को हनुमान कहते हैं

दुनिया के मालिक को भगवान कहते हैं
दुनिया के मालिक को भगवान कहते हैं
संकट के साथी को हनुमान कहते हैं
संकट के साथी को हनुमान कहते हैं

दिल से जो इनकी भक्ति करेगा
हनुमान उसका साथी बनेगा

हनुमान उसका साथी बनेगा
हनुमान उसका साथी बनेगा

बनवारी जो भी शरण में रहेगा
ये उसका बेड़ा पार करेगा

ये उसका बेड़ा पार करेगा
ये उसका बेड़ा पार करेगा

इनके बारे में
इनके बारे में श्रीराम कहते हैं
इनके बारे में श्रीराम कहते हैं

संकट के साथी को हनुमान कहते हैं
संकट के साथी को हनुमान कहते हैं
दुनिया के मालिक को भगवान कहते हैं
दुनिया के मालिक को भगवान कहते हैं
संकट के साथी को हनुमान कहते हैं
संकट के साथी को हनुमान कहते हैं

Duniya Ke Malik Ko Bhagwan Kehte Hai

Duniya Ke Malik Ko Bhagwan Kehte Hai

Duniya Ke Malik Ko Bhagwan Kehte Hai

Sankat Ke Saathi Ko Hanuman Kehte Hain

Sankat Ke Saathi Ko Hanuman Kehte Hain

Duniya Ke Malik Ko Bhagwan Kehte Hai

Sankat Ke Saathi Ko Hanuman Kehte Hain

Jab Rishtedaar Tumase Mukhadaa Chhupaye

Hanuman Tera Saath Nibhaye

Hanuman Tera Saath Nibhaye

Hanuman Tera Saath Nibhaye

Jab Duniya Wale De Naa Sahaara

Hanuman Pakde Daaman Tumhaara

Hanuman Pakde Daaman Tumhaara

Hanuman Pakde Daaman Tumhaara

Padh Lo Saare

Padh Lo Saare Ved Aur Puraan Kehte Hain

Padh Lo Saare Ved Aur Puraan Kehte Hain

Sankat Ke Saathi Ko Hanuman Kehte Hain

Sankat Ke Saathi Ko Hanuman Kehte Hain

Duniya Ke Malik Ko Bhagwan Kehte Hai

Duniya Ke Malik Ko Bhagwan Kehte Hai

Sankat Ke Saathi Ko Hanuman Kehte Hain

Sankat Ke Saathi Ko Hanuman Kehte Hain

Jo Kaam Iske Vash Mein Nahin Hai

Ek Kaam Humko Aisa Bataa Do

Ek Kaam Humko Aisa Bataa Do

Ek Kaam Humko Aisa Bataa Do

Hanuman Khush Ho Jayega Tumase

Bas Inko Thoda Sindoor Laga Do

Bas Inko Thoda Sindoor Laga Do

Bas Inko Thoda Sindoor Laga Do

Duniya Ke

Duniya Ke Saare Insaan Kehte Hain

Duniya Ke Saare Insaan Kehte Hain

Sankat Ke Saathi Ko Hanuman Kehte Hain

Sankat Ke Saathi Ko Hanuman Kehte Hain

Duniya Ke Malik Ko Bhagwan Kehte Hai

Duniya Ke Malik Ko Bhagwan Kehte Hai

Sankat Ke Saathi Ko Hanuman Kehte Hain

Sankat Ke Saathi Ko Hanuman Kehte Hain

Dil Se Jo Inki Bhakti Karega

Hanuman Uskaa Saathi Banega

Hanuman Uskaa Saathi Banega

Hanuman Uska Saathi Banega

'Banavaari' Jo Bhi Sharan Mein Rahega

Ye Uskaa Beda Paar Karegaa

Ye Uskaa Beda Paar Karega

Ye Uskaa Beda Paar Karega

Inake Baare Mein

Inake Baare Mein Shri Ram Kehte Hain

Inake Baare Mein Shriram Kehte Hain

Sankat Ke Saathi Ko Hanuman Kehte Hain

Sankat Ke Saathi Ko Hanuman Kehte Hain

Duniya Ke Malik Ko Bhagwan Kehte Hai

Duniya Ke Malik Ko Bhagwan Kehte Hai

Sankat Ke Saathi Ko Hanuman Kehte Hain

Sankat Ke Saathi Ko Hanuman Kehte Hain

जिनके मन में बसे श्री राम जी

जिनके मन में बसे श्री राम जी
उनकी रक्षा करें हनुमान जी
जिनके मन में बसे श्री राम जी

जब भक्तों पर विपदा आई
तब आये हनुमंत गोसाई
कृपा राम भक्तो पर करते
उनकी पीड़ा को हर लेते
जय कपीष बलवान की

उनकी रक्षा करें हनुमान जी
जिनके मन में बसे श्री राम जी
उनकी रक्षा करें हनुमान जी
जिनके मन में बसे श्री राम जी

राम कथा के अद्‌बुत नायक
रामदूत भक्तो के सहायक
जय जय जय प्रभु हितकारी
ध्यान करूँ नित मंगलकारी
दे दो शरण हनुमान जी

उनकी रक्षा करें हनुमान जी
जिनके मन में बसे श्री राम जी
उनकी रक्षा करें हनुमान जी
जिनके मन में बसे श्री राम जी

भक्ति जहाँ श्री राम की होती
शक्ति वहां हनुमान की होती
विघ्न काल सब दूर मिटाते
मनोकामना पूर्ण कराते
जय बजरंग महान की

उनकी रक्षा करें हनुमान जी
जिनके मन में बसे श्री राम जी
उनकी रक्षा करें हनुमान जी
जिनके मन में बसे श्री राम जी

निशदिन करूँ तुम्हारी पूजा
तुम सम हनुमत कोई ना दूजा
बदन सिंदुरी जय कपीष जय
सन्मुख रहो, झुकाऊँ शीश मैं
जय जय कृपा निधान की

उनकी रक्षा करें हनुमान जी
जिनके मन में बसे श्री राम जी
उनकी रक्षा करें हनुमान जी
जिनके मन में बसे श्री राम जी

जिनके मन में बसे श्री राम जी
उनकी रक्षा करें हनुमान जी

Jinke Man Me Base Shri Ramji

Jinke Man Me Base Shri Ramji

Unki Raksha Kare Hanumanji

Jinke Man Me Base Shri Ramji

Jab Bhakton Par Vipada Aai

Tab Aaye Hanumant Gosai

Kripa Ram Bhakto Par Karate

Unki Pida Ko Har Lete

Jay Kapish Balwaan Ki

Unki Raksha Kare Hanumanji

Jinke Man Me Base Shri Ramji

Unki Raksha Kare Hanumanji

Jinke Man Me Base Shri Ramji

Ram Katha Ke Adbut Naayak

Raam-Doot Bhakto Ke Sahaayak

Jay Jay Jay Prabhu Hitkaari

Dhyaan Karu Nit Mangal-Kaari

De Do Sharan Hanumanji

Unki Raksha Kare Hanumanji

Jinke Man Me Base Shri Ramji

Unki Raksha Kare Hanumanji

Jinke Man Me Base Shri Ramji

Bhakti Jahaan Shri Ram Ki Hoti

Shakti Wahaa Hanuman Ki Hoti

Vighna Kaal Sab Door Mitaate

Manokaamana Poorna Karaate

Jay Bajarang Mahaan Ki

Unki Raksha Kare Hanumanji

Jinke Man Me Base Shri Ramji

Unki Raksha Kare Hanumanji

Jinke Man Me Base Shri Ramji

Nishadin Karu Tumhaari Pooja

Tum Sam Hanumat Koi Na Dooja

Badan Sinduri Jay Kapish Jay

Sanmukh Raho, Jhukaoo Shish Main

Jay Jay Kripa Nidhaan Ki

Unki Raksha Kare Hanumanji

Jinke Man Me Base Shri Ramji

Unki Raksha Kare Hanumanji

Jinke Man Me Base Shri Ramji

Jinke Man Me Base Shri Ramji

Unki Raksha Kare Hanumanji

आज्ञा नहीं है माँ मुझे

आज्ञा नहीं है माँ मुझे
किसी और काम की
वरना भुजाएँ तोड़ दूँ
सौगंध राम की

आज्ञा नहीं है माँ मुझे
किसी और काम की

लंका पाताल ठोक दूँ
रावण के शान की
चाहूँ तो भीख मांगे ये
दानव भी प्राण की

सोने की लंका जला दूँ
सौगंध राम की

आज्ञा नहीं है माँ मुझे
किसी और काम की

ना झूठी शान करू
ना अभिमान करू
प्रभु का ध्यान धरु
राम गुण गान करू

सच्चे दया के सागर है वो
रघुकुल की शान है
बल हूँ मै, बल के धाम वो
सौगंध राम की

आज्ञा नहीं है माँ मुझे
किसी और काम की

विश्वास करलो माँ मेरा
आयेंगे राम जी

रावण को दंड दे कर
ले जायेंगे राम जी
तब तक न खोना धैर्य माँ
तुम्हे सौगंध राम की

आज्ञा नहीं है माँ मुझे
किसी और काम की

रावण को मार कर प्रभु
बैठे विमान पर

बोली यु सीता कर कृपा
अंजनी के लाल पर
हनुमान ने कहा जो कर दिया
सौगंध राम की

आज्ञा नहीं है माँ मुझे
किसी और काम की

Aagya Nahi Hai Maa Mujhe

Aagya Nahi Hai Maa Mujhe

Kisi Aur Kaam Ki

Varna Bhujaye Tod Doo

Saugandh Ram Ki

Aagya Nahi Hai Maa Mujhe

Kisi Aur Kaam Ki

Lanka Paataal Thok Doo

Raavan Ke Shaan Ki

Chaahoon To Bhikh Maange Ye

Daanav Bhi Praan Ki

Sone Ki Lanka Jala Doo

Saugandh Raam Ki

Aagya Nahi Hai Maa Mujhe
Kisi Aur Kaam Ki

Na Jhoothi Shaan Karoo
Na Abhimaan Karoo
Prabhu Ka Dhyaan Dharu
Raam Gun Gaan Karoo

Sachche Daya Ke Saagar Hai Vo
Raghukul Ki Shaan Hai
Bal Hoon Mai, Bal Ke Dhaam Vo
Saugandh Raam Ki

Aagya Nahi Hai Maa Mujhe
Kisi Aur Kaam Ki

Vishvaas Kar Lo Maa Mera
Aayenge Raamji

Raavan Ko Dand De Kar

Le Jaayenge Ramji

Tab Tak Na Khona Dhairya Maa

Tumhe Saugandh Ram Ki

Aagya Nahi Hai Maa Mujhe

Kisi Aur Kaam Ki

Raavan Ko Maar Kar Prabhu

Baithe Vimaan Par

Boli Yu Sita Kar Kripa

Anjani Ke Laal Par

Hanuman Ne Kaha Jo Kar Diya

Saugandh Ram Ki

Aagya Nahi Hai Maa Mujhe

Kisi Aur Kaam Ki

हे दुःख भन्जन, मारुती नंदन

हे दुःख भन्जन, मारुती नंदन
सुन लो मेरी पुकार
पवनसुत विनती बारम्बार

अष्ट सिद्धि नव निधि के दाता
दुखियों के तुम भाग्यविधाता
सियाराम के काज संवारे
मेरा कर उद्धार

पवनसुत विनती बारम्बार
पवनसुत विनती बारम्बार

हे दुःख भन्जन, मारुती नंदन
सुन लो मेरी पुकार
पवनसुत विनती बारम्बार
पवनसुत विनती बारम्बार

अपरम्पार है शक्ति तुम्हारी
तुम पर रीझे अवधबिहारी
भक्ति भाव से ध्याऊं तोहे
कर दुखों से पार

पवनसुत विनती बारम्बार
पवनसुत विनती बारम्बार

हे दुःख भन्जन, मारुती नंदन
सुन लो मेरी पुकार
पवनसुत विनती बारम्बार
पवनसुत विनती बारम्बार

जपूँ निरंतर नाम तिहारा
अब नहीं छोड़ूं तेरा द्वारा
राम भक्त मोहे शरण मे लीजे
भाव सागर से तार

पवनसुत विनती बारम्बार
पवनसुत विनती बारम्बार

हे दुःख भन्जन, मारुती नंदन
सुन लो मेरी पुकार
पवनसुत विनती बारम्बार
पवनसुत विनती बारम्बार

हे दुःख भन्जन, मारुती नंदन
सुन लो मेरी पुकार
पवनसुत विनती बारम्बार
पवनसुत विनती बारम्बार

Hey Dukh Bhanjan Maruti Nandan

Hey Dukh Bhanjan Maruti Nandan

Sun Lo Meri Pukaar

Pawansut Vinti Barambar

Asht Siddhi Nav Nidhi Ke Daata

Dukhiyon Ke Tum Bhaagya-Vidhaata

Siyaram Ke Kaaj Sanvaare

Mera Kar Uddhaar

Pawansut Vinti Barambar

Pawansut Vinti Barambar

Hey Dukh Bhanjan Maruti Nandan

Sun Lo Meri Pukaar

Pawansut Vinti Barambar

Pawansut Vinti Barambar

Aparampaar Hai Shakti Tumhaari

Tum Par Rijhe Awadhbihaari

Bhakti Bhaav Se Dhyaau Tohe

Kar Dukhon Se Paar

Pawansut Vinti Barambar

Pawansut Vinti Barambar

Hey Dukh Bhanjan Maruti Nandan

Sun Lo Meri Pukaar

Pawansut Vinti Barambar

Pawansut Vinti Barambar

Japoon Nirantar Naam Tihaara

Ab Nahin Chhodoon Tera Dwara

Ram Bhakt Mohe Sharan Me Lije

Bhaav Sagar Se Taar

Pawansut Vinti Barambar

Pawansut Vinti Barambar

Hey Dukh Bhanjan Maruti Nandan

Sun Lo Meri Pukaar

Pawansut Vinti Barambar

Pawansut Vinti Barambar

Hey Dukh Bhanjan Maruti Nandan

Sun Lo Meri Pukaar

Pawansut Vinti Barambar

Pawansut Vinti Barambar

आ जाओ तेरा सजा दिया दरबार बालाजी

आ जाओ आ जाओ
तेरा सजा दिया दरबार
बालाजी आ जाओ

गौरी नन्द गणेश बुलाये
ब्रह्मा विष्णु महेश भी आये
माँ गोरा हो रही तैयार
बालाजी आ जाओ

आ जाओ आ जाओ
तेरा सजा दिया दरबार
बालाजी आ जाओ

श्री राम आवे मैया जानकी
सरस्वती दे राह ज्ञान की

माँ संग में राखे सितार

बालाजी आ जाओ

आ जाओ आ जाओ

तेरा सजा दिया दरबार

बालाजी आ जाओ

राधा रुक्मण आवे कृष्ण

काली वैष्णो के हो जा दर्शन

आवे शिवजी राज सरकार

बालाजी आ जाओ

आ जाओ आ जाओ

तेरा सजा दिया दरबार

बालाजी आ जाओ

सारे देवता आये सत्संग में

सारे भक्त आवे उमंग में

गावे भक्त गीत मल्हार

बालाजी आ जाओ

आ जाओ आ जाओ

तेरा सजा दिया दरबार

बालाजी आ जाओ

आ जाओ, आ जाओ

तेरा सजा दिया दरबार

बालाजी आ जाओ

Aa Jao Tera Saja Diya Darbar Balaji

Aa Jao Aa Jao

Tera Saja Diya Darbar

Balaji Aa Jao

Gauri Nand Ganesh Bulaaye

Brahma Vishnu Mahesh Bhee Aaye

Maa Gaura Ho Rahi Taiyaar

Balaji Aa Jao

Aa Jao Aa Jao

Tera Saja Diya Darbar

Balaji Aa Jao

Shree Ram Aave Maiya Jaanaki

Saraswati De Raah Gyaan Ki

Maan Sang Mein Raakhe Sitaar

Balaji Aa Jao

Aa Jao Aa Jao

Tera Saja Diya Darbar

Balaji Aa Jao

Raadha Rukmani Aave Krshn

Kaali Vaishno Ke Ho Ja Darshan

Aave Shivajee Raaj Sarakaar

Balaji Aa Jao

Aa Jao Aa Jao

Tera Saja Diya Darbar

Balaji Aa Jao

Saare Devata Aaye Satsang Mein

Saare Bhakt Aave Umang Mein

Gaave Bhakt Geet Malhaar

Balaji Aa Jao

Aa Jao Aa Jao

Tera Saja Diya Darbar

Balaji Aa Jao

Aa Jao Aa Jao

Tera Saja Diya Darbar

Balaji Aa Jao